Floral Mandala Coloring Book

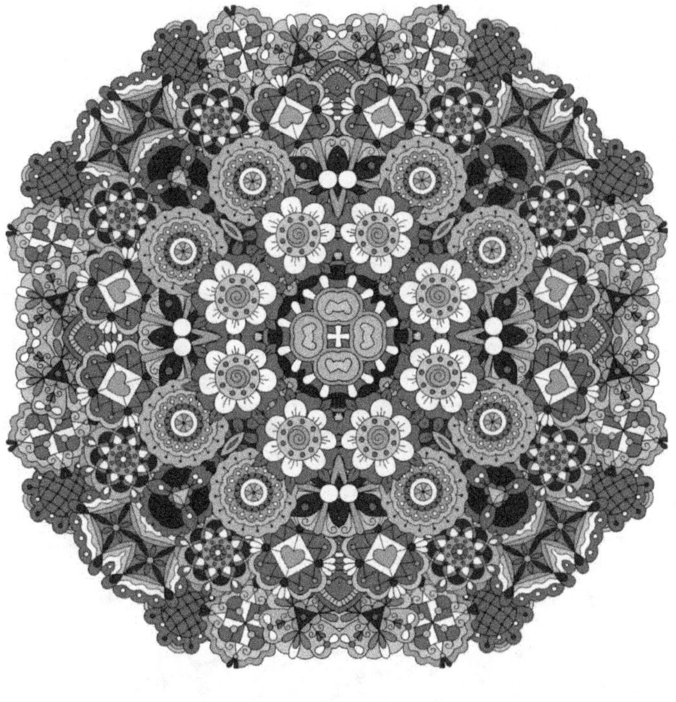

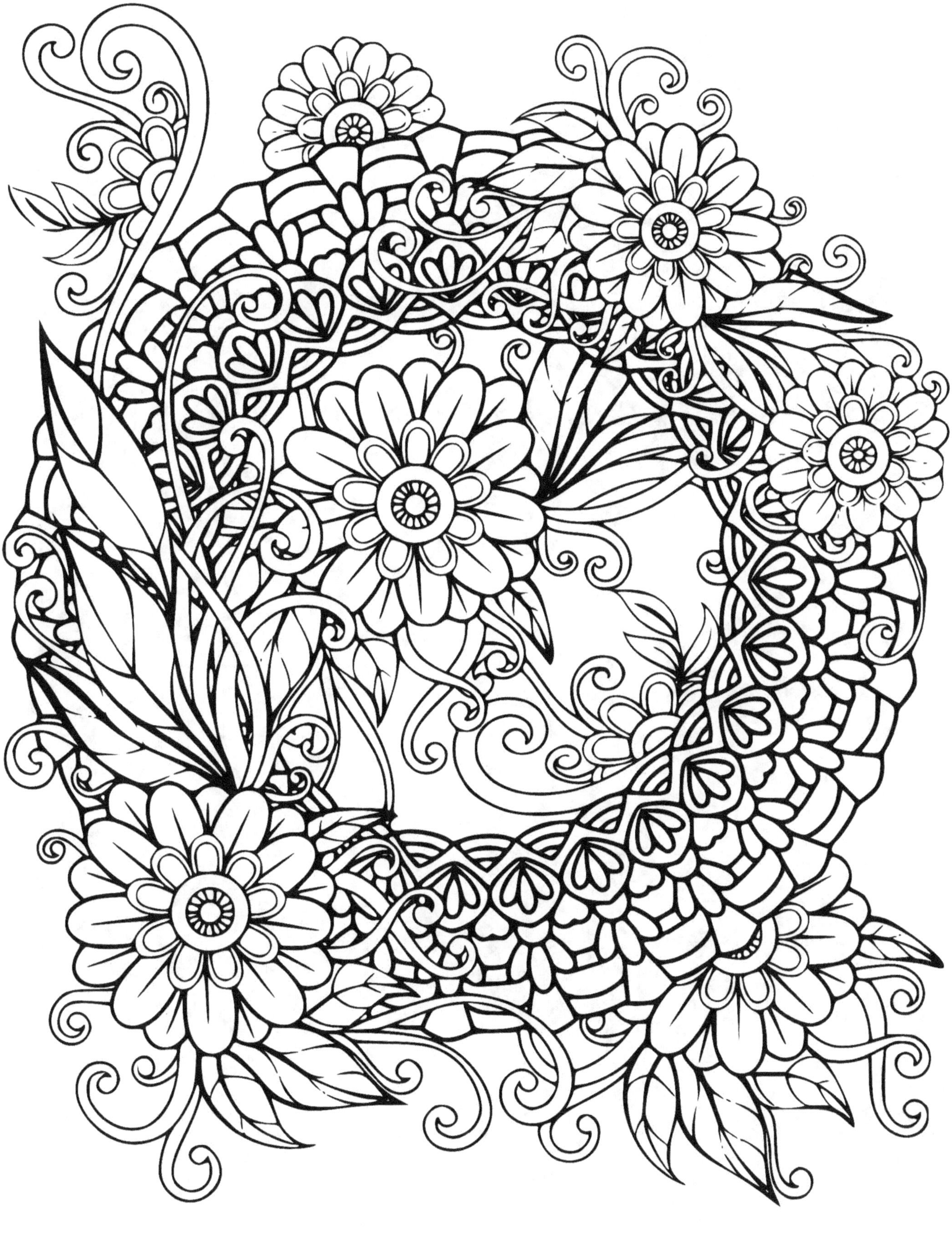

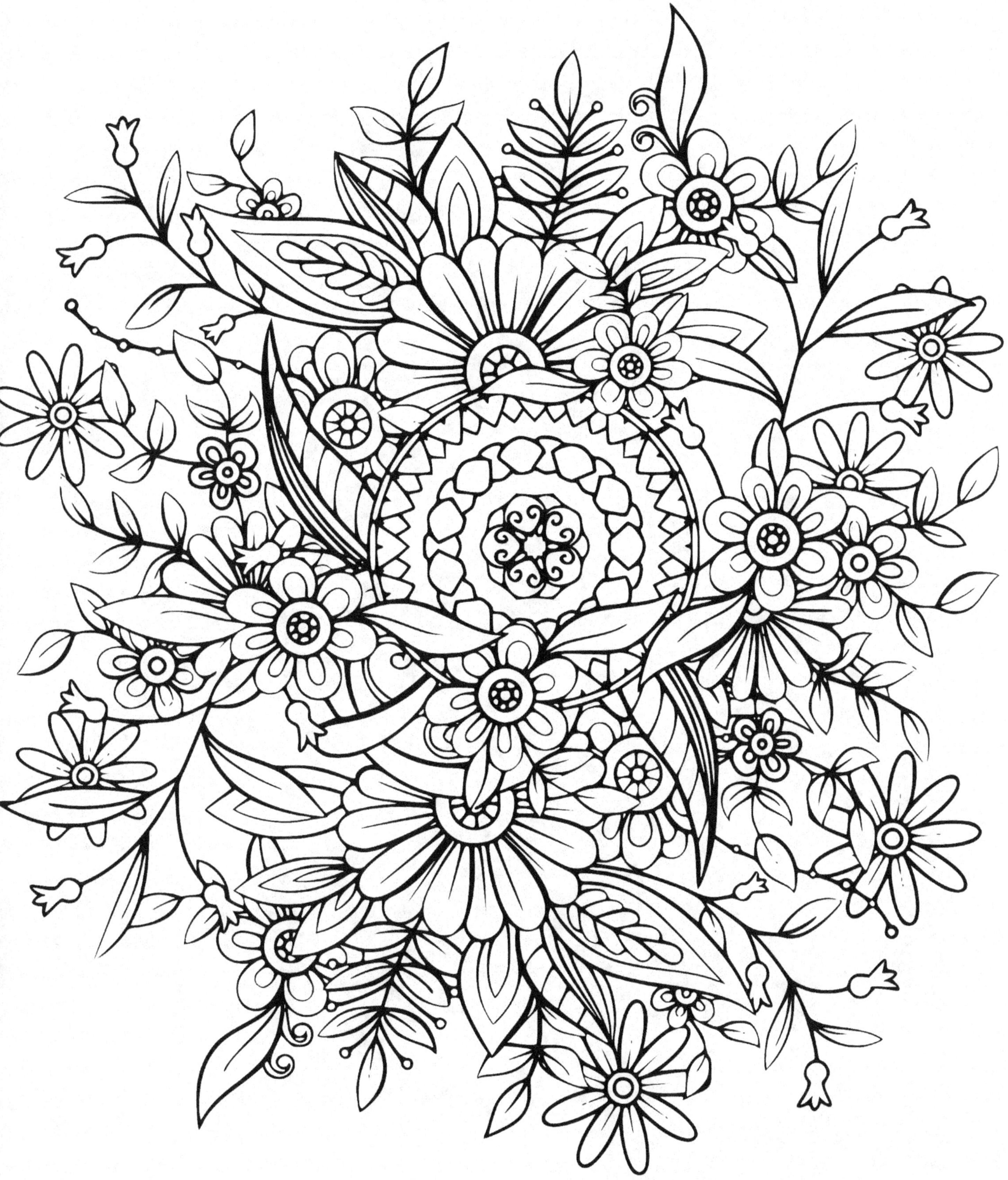

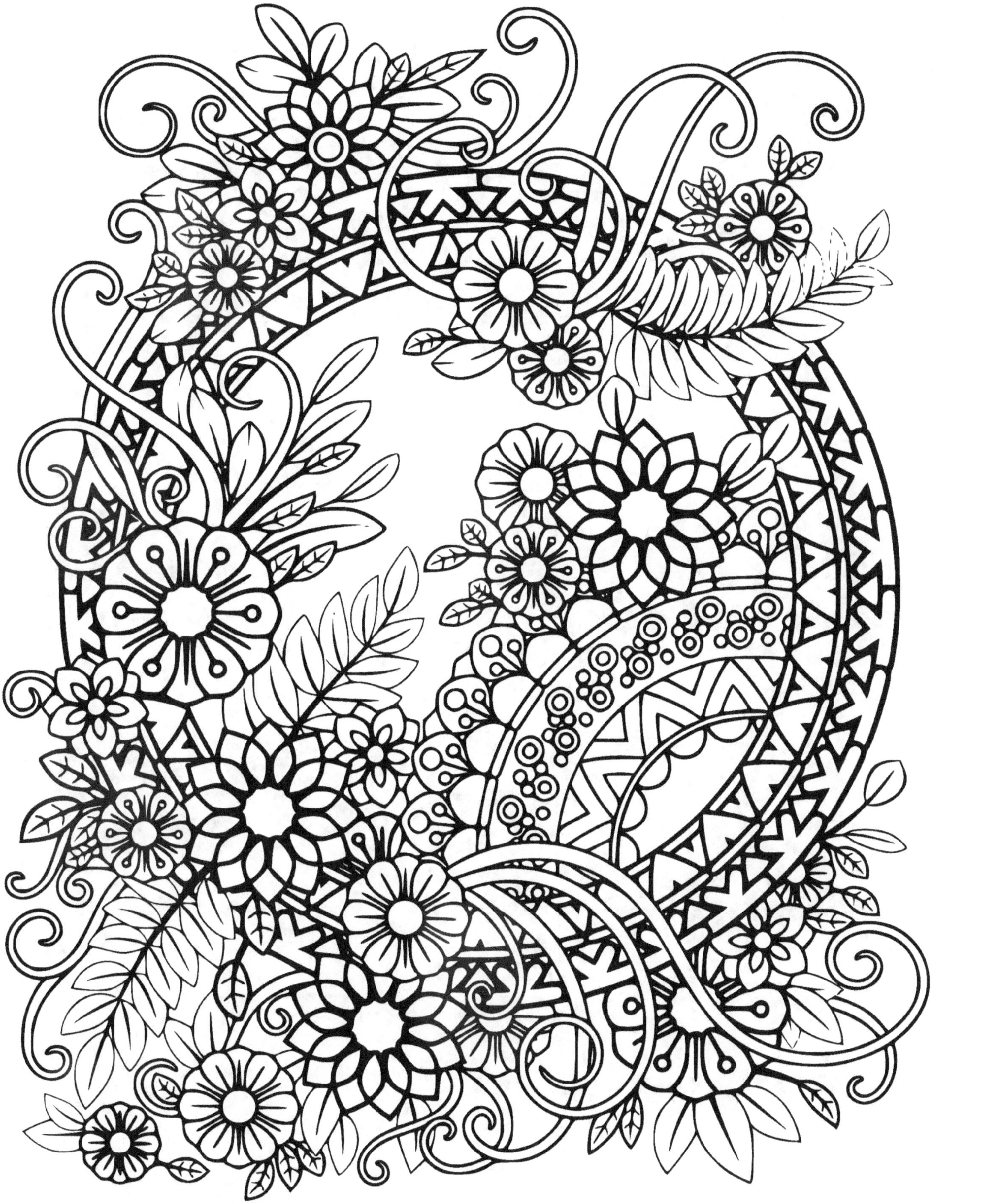

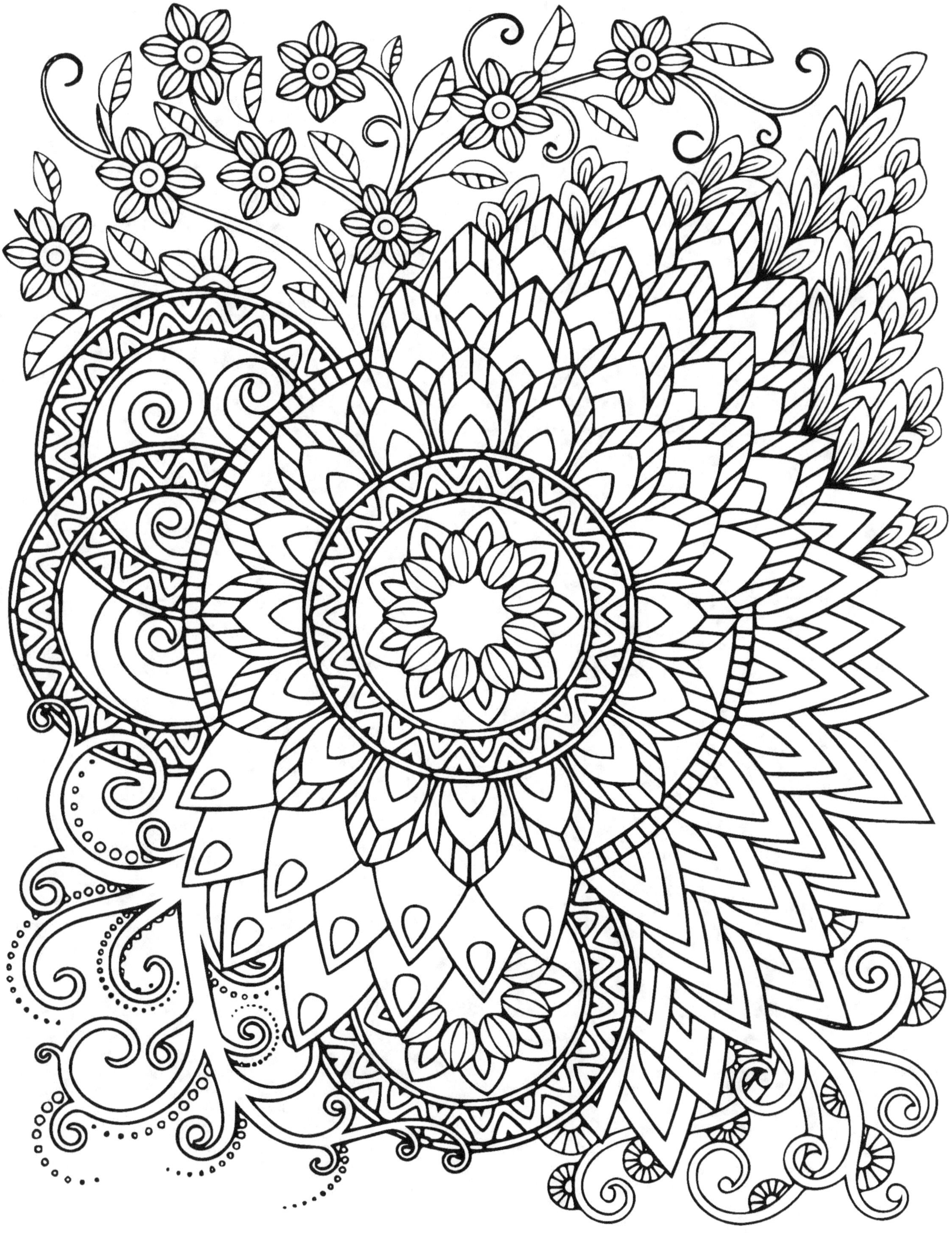

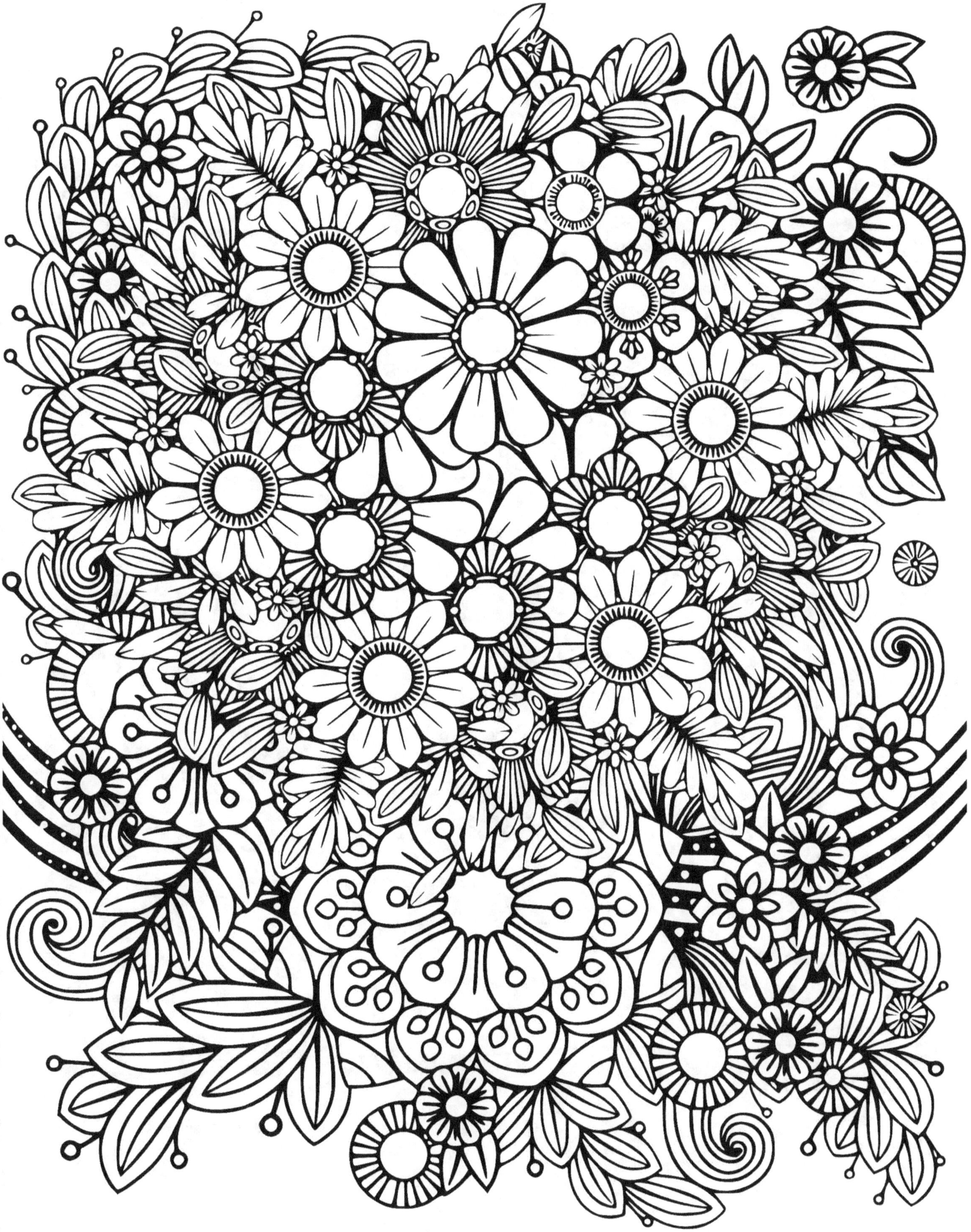

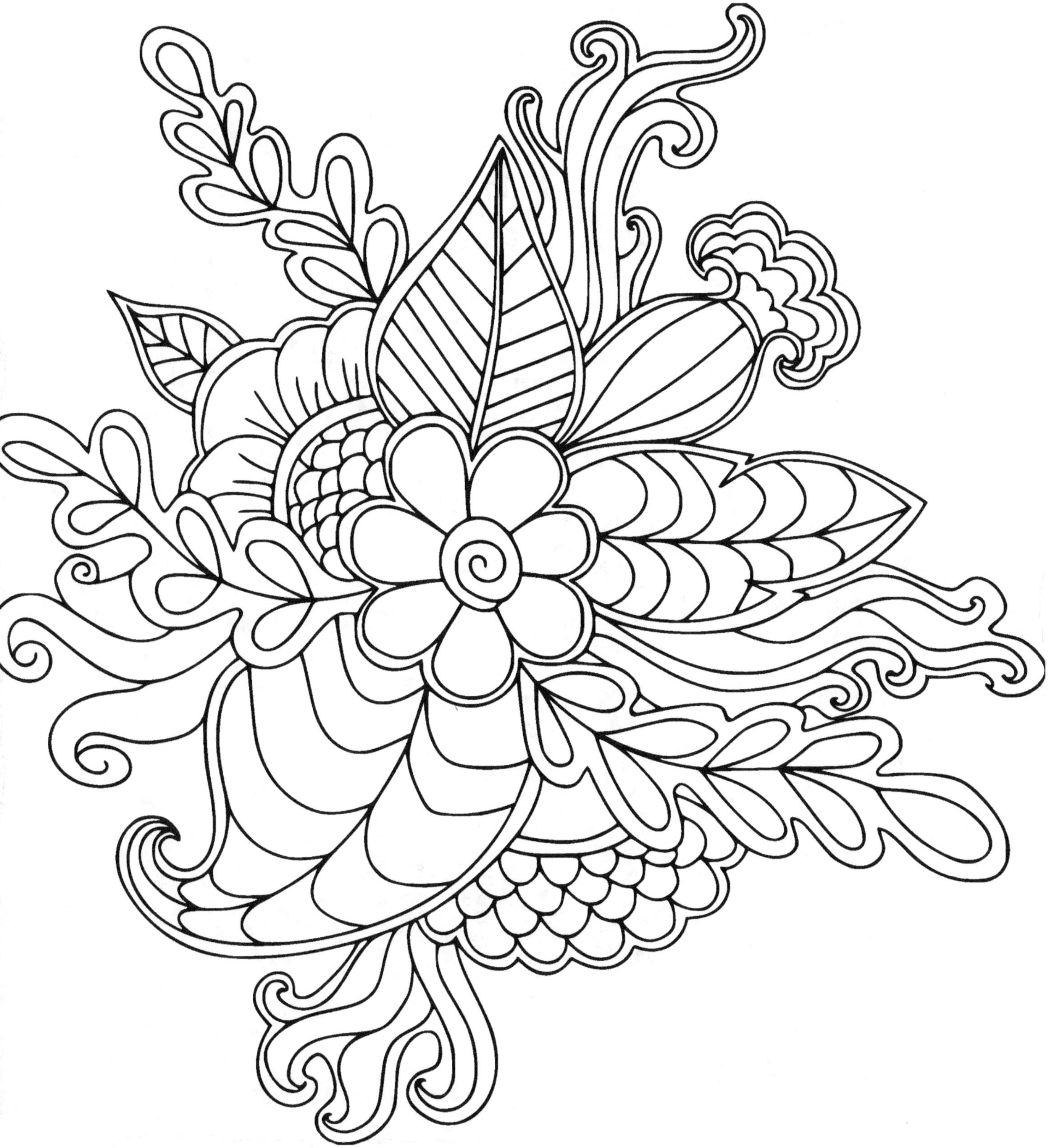

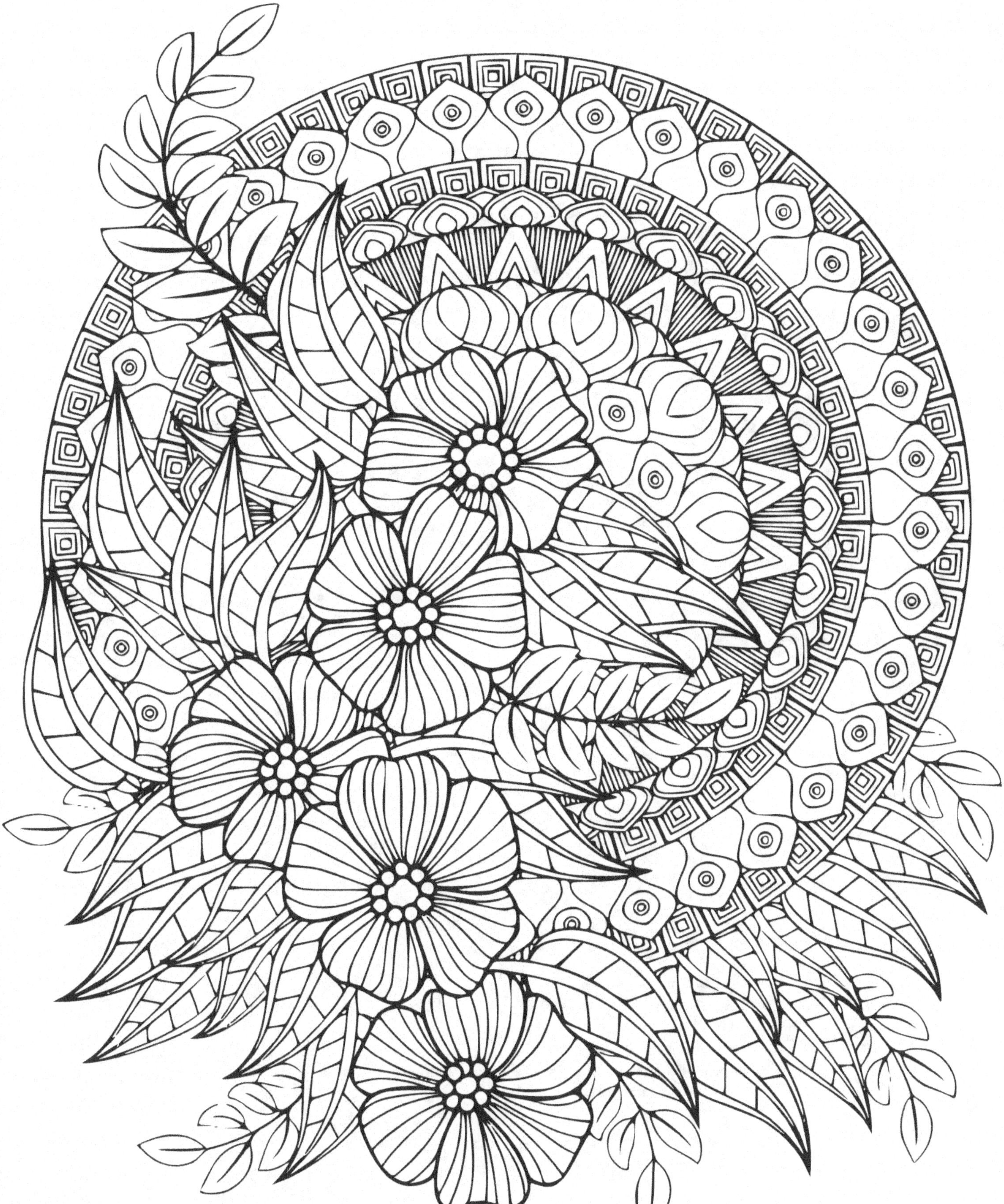

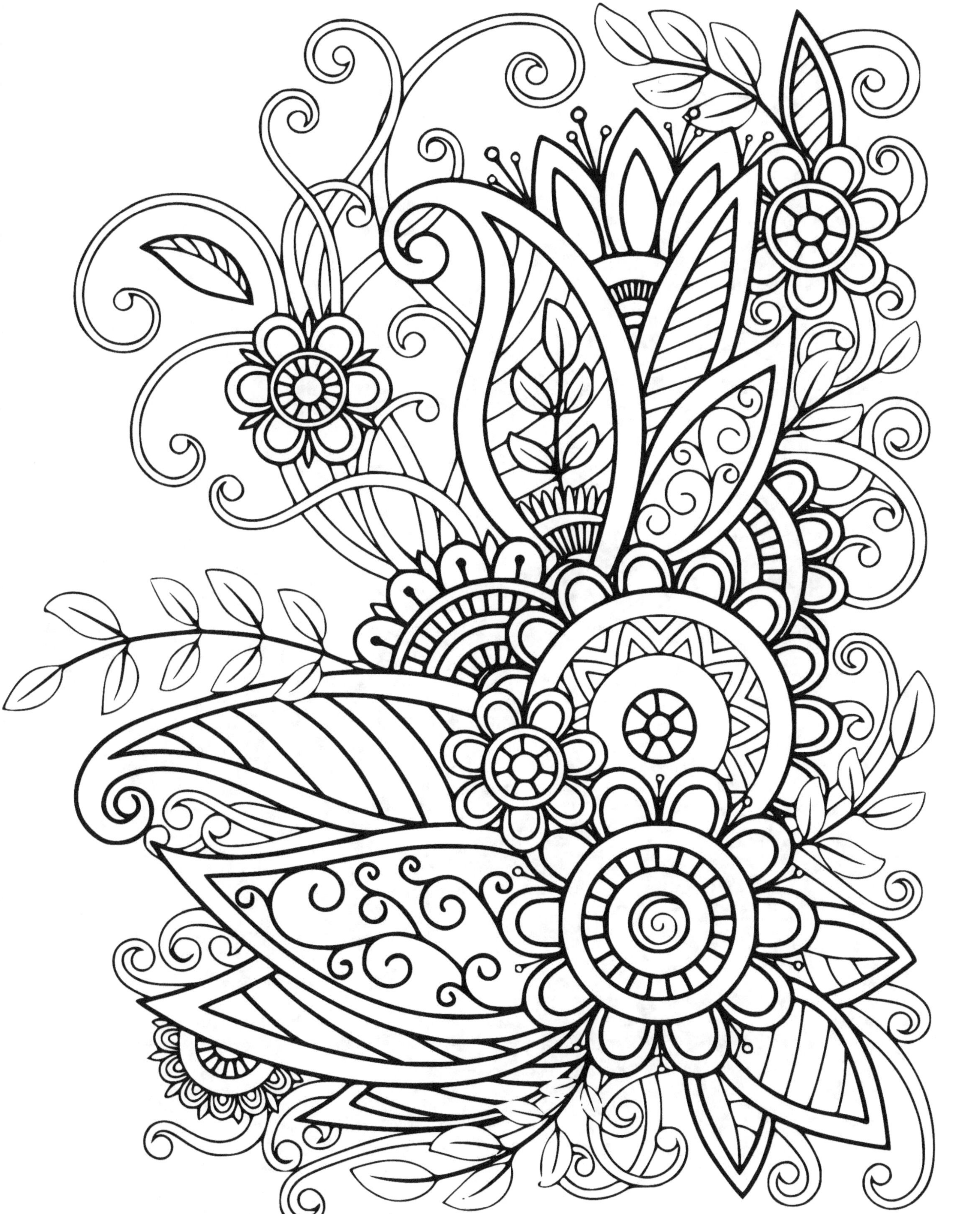

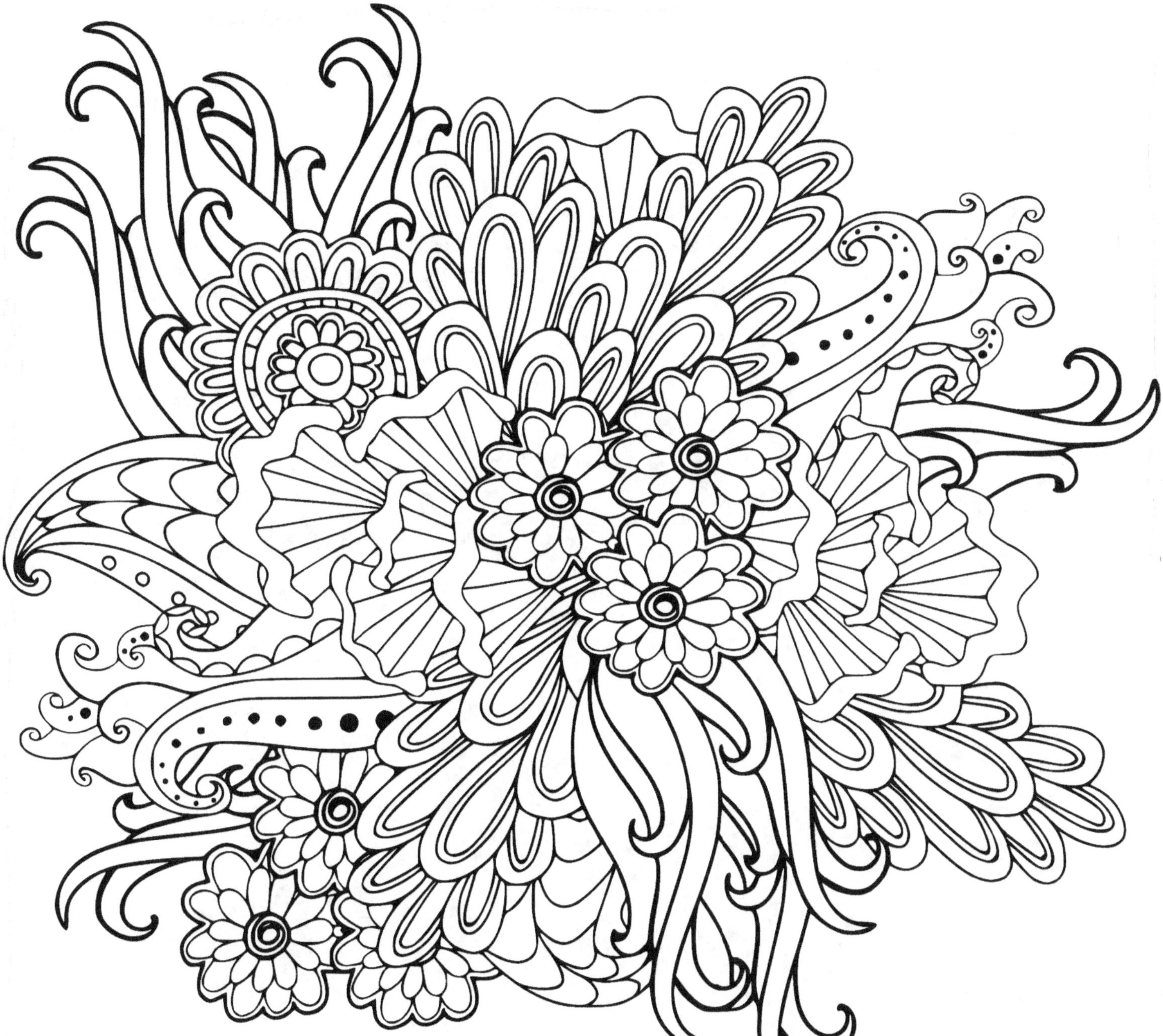

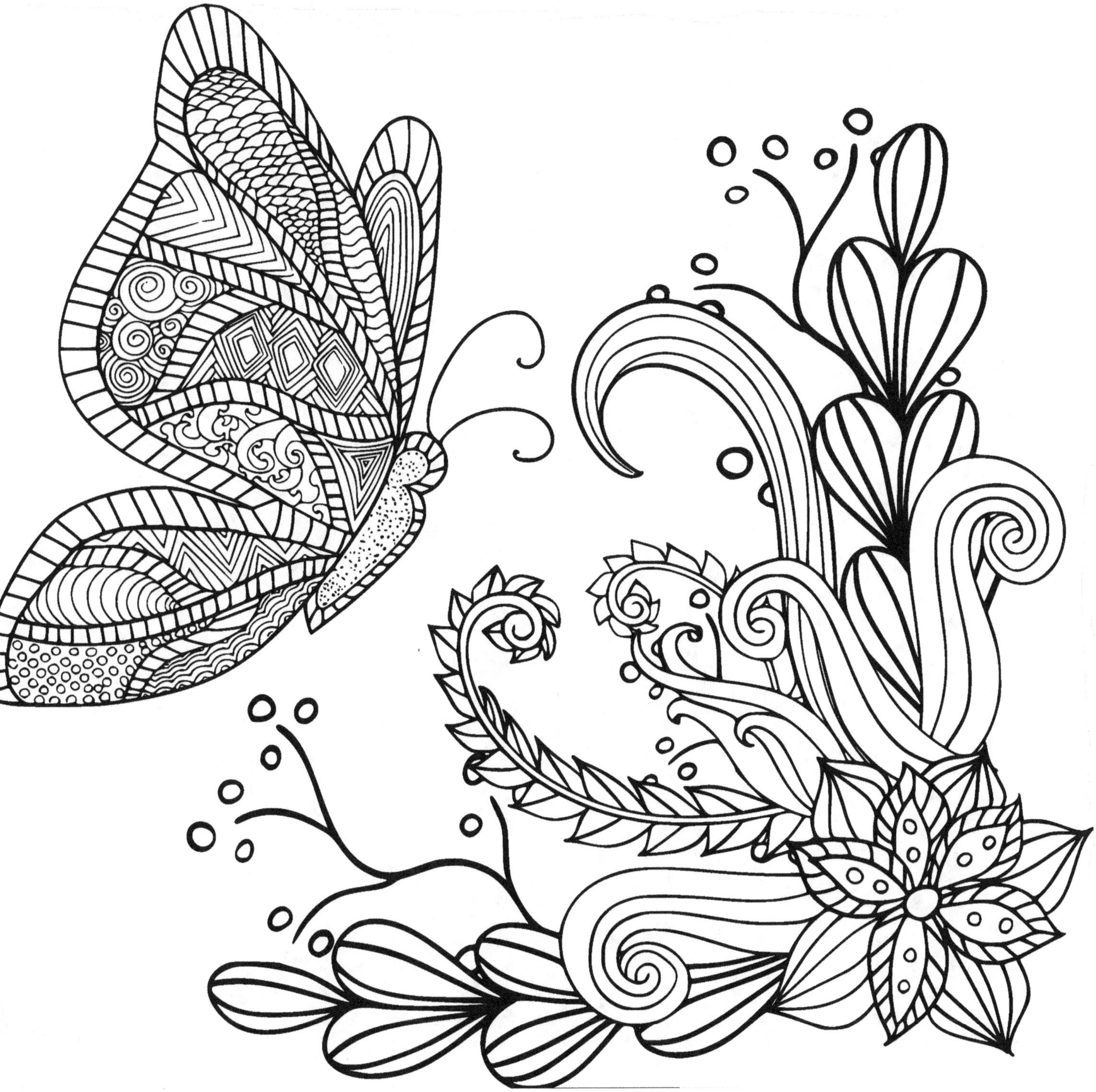

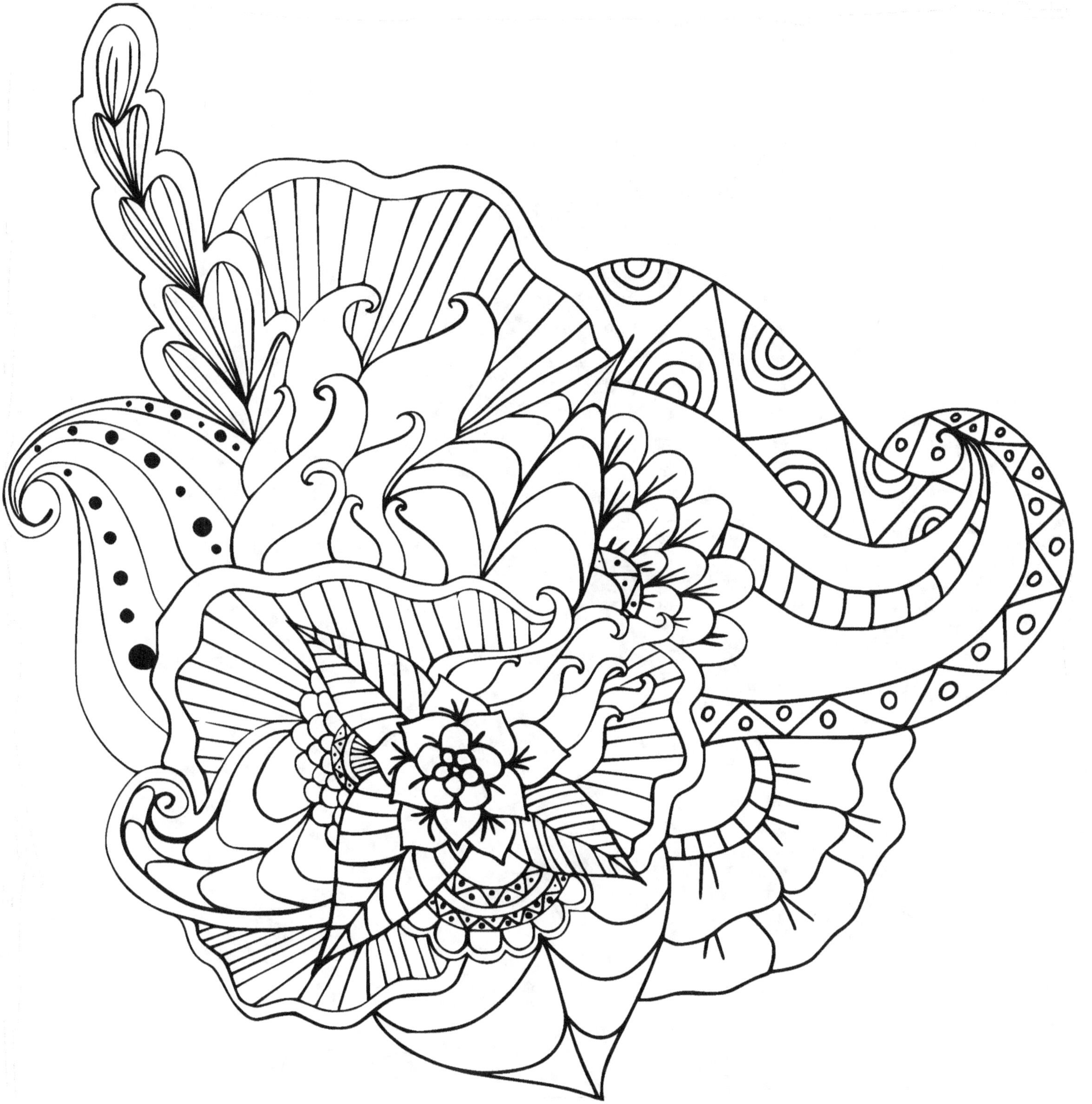

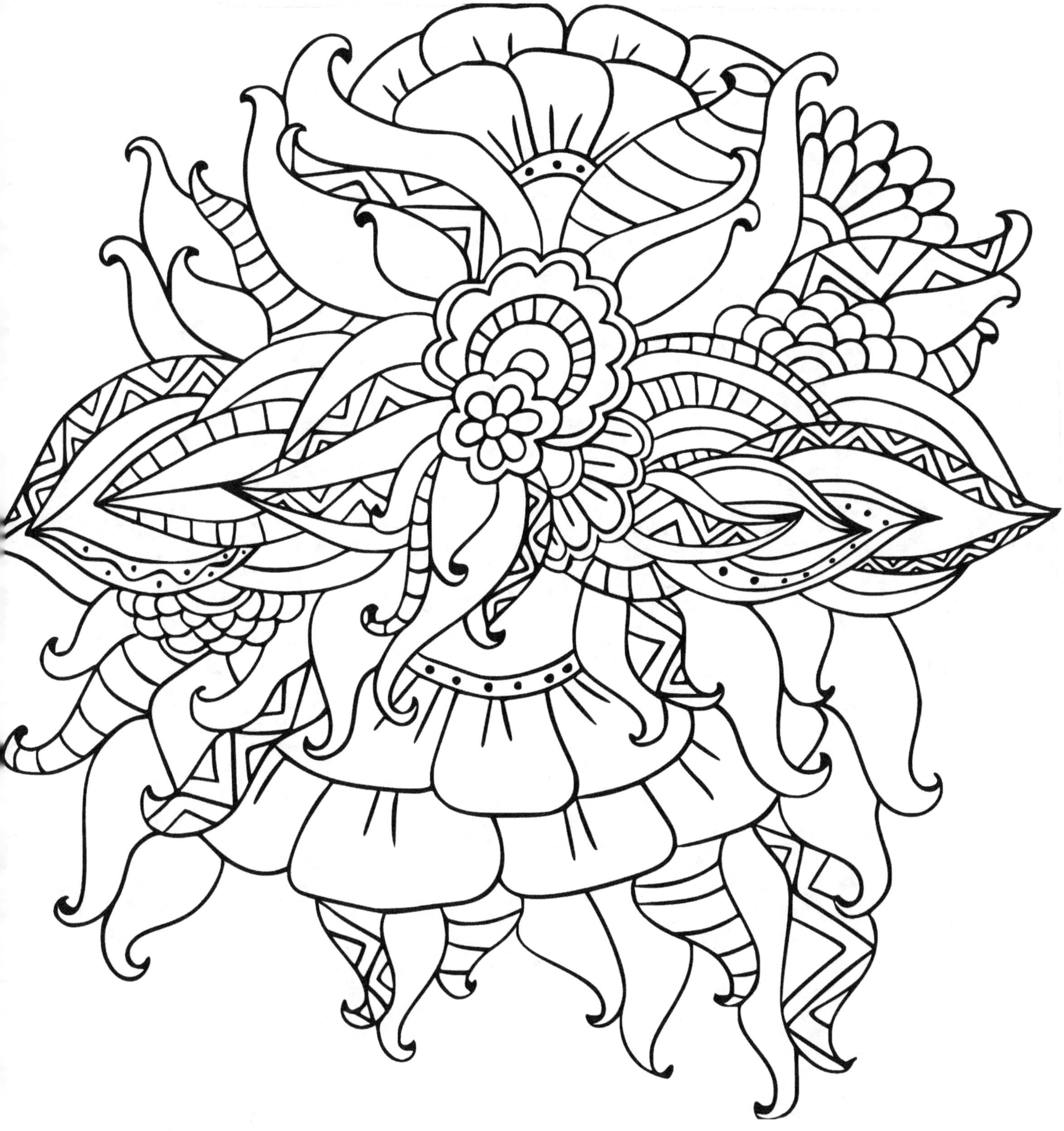

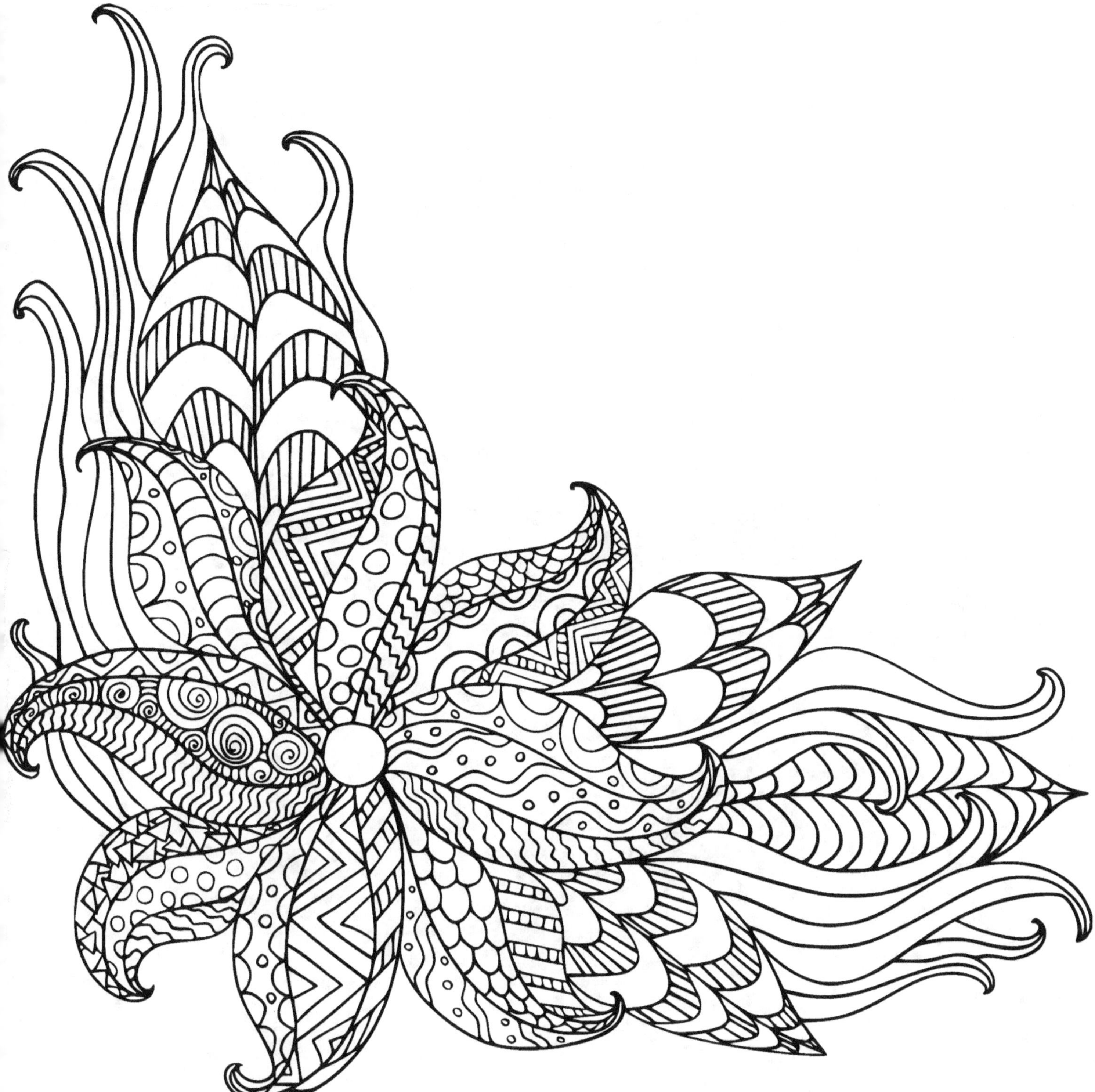

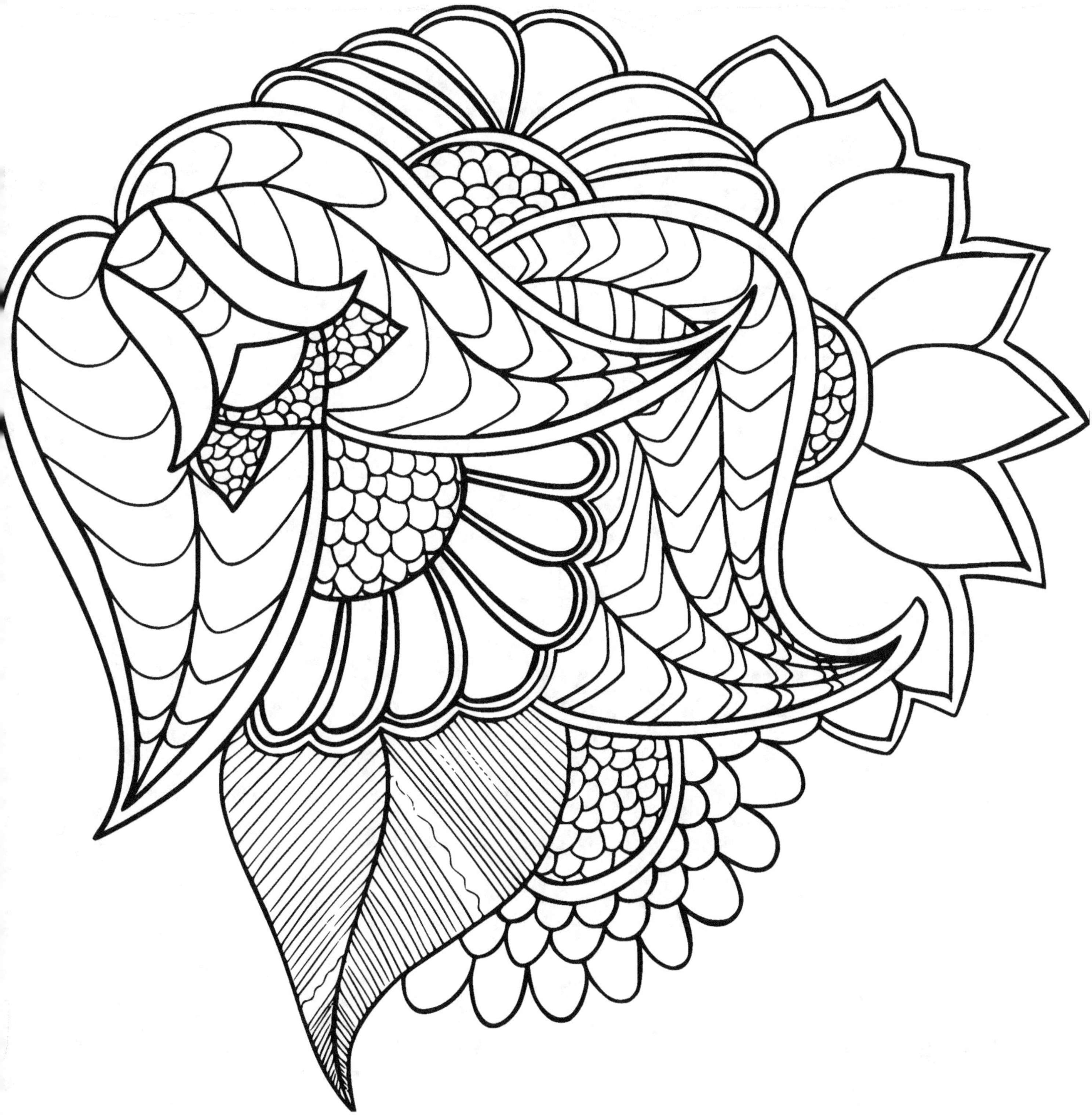

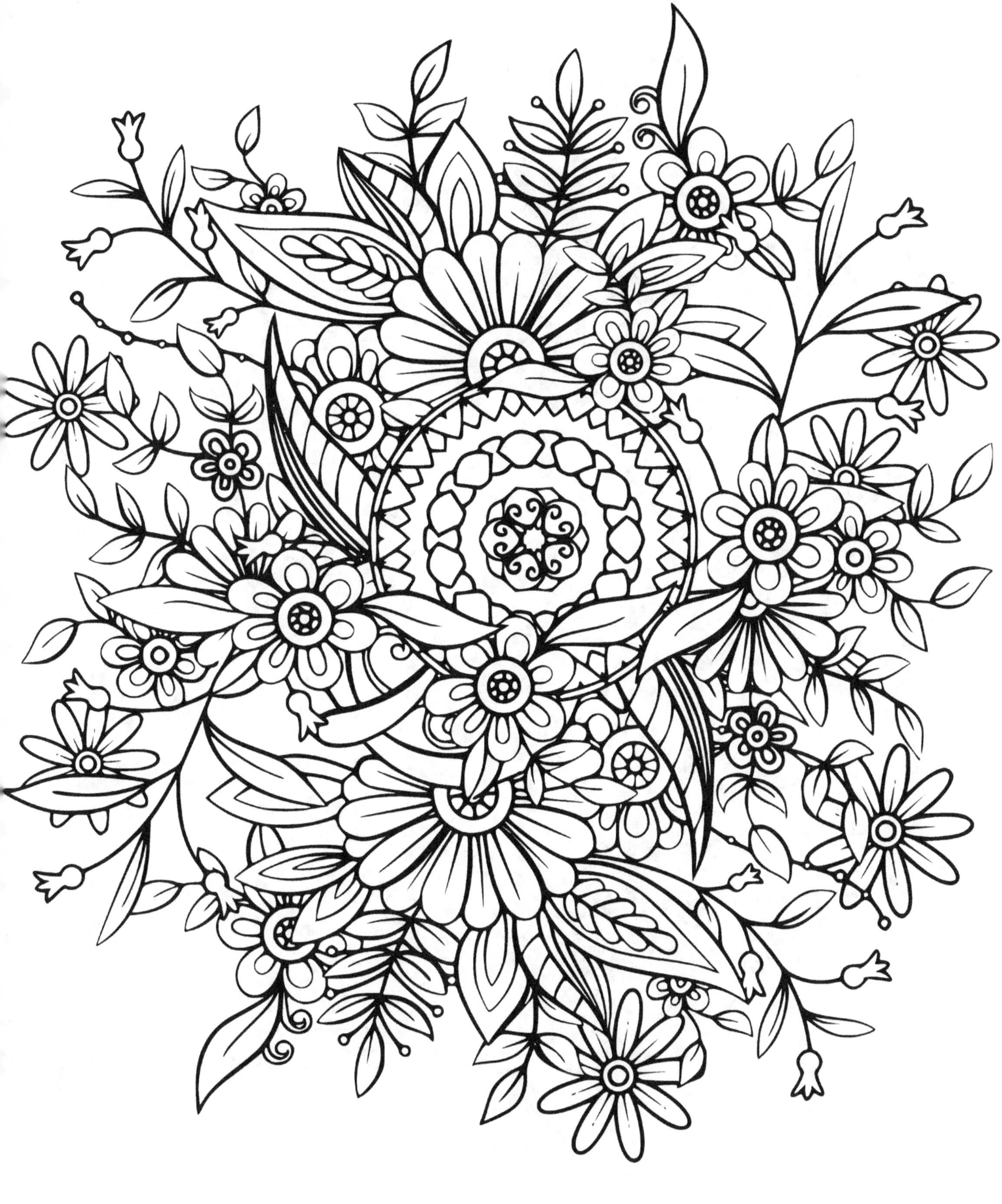

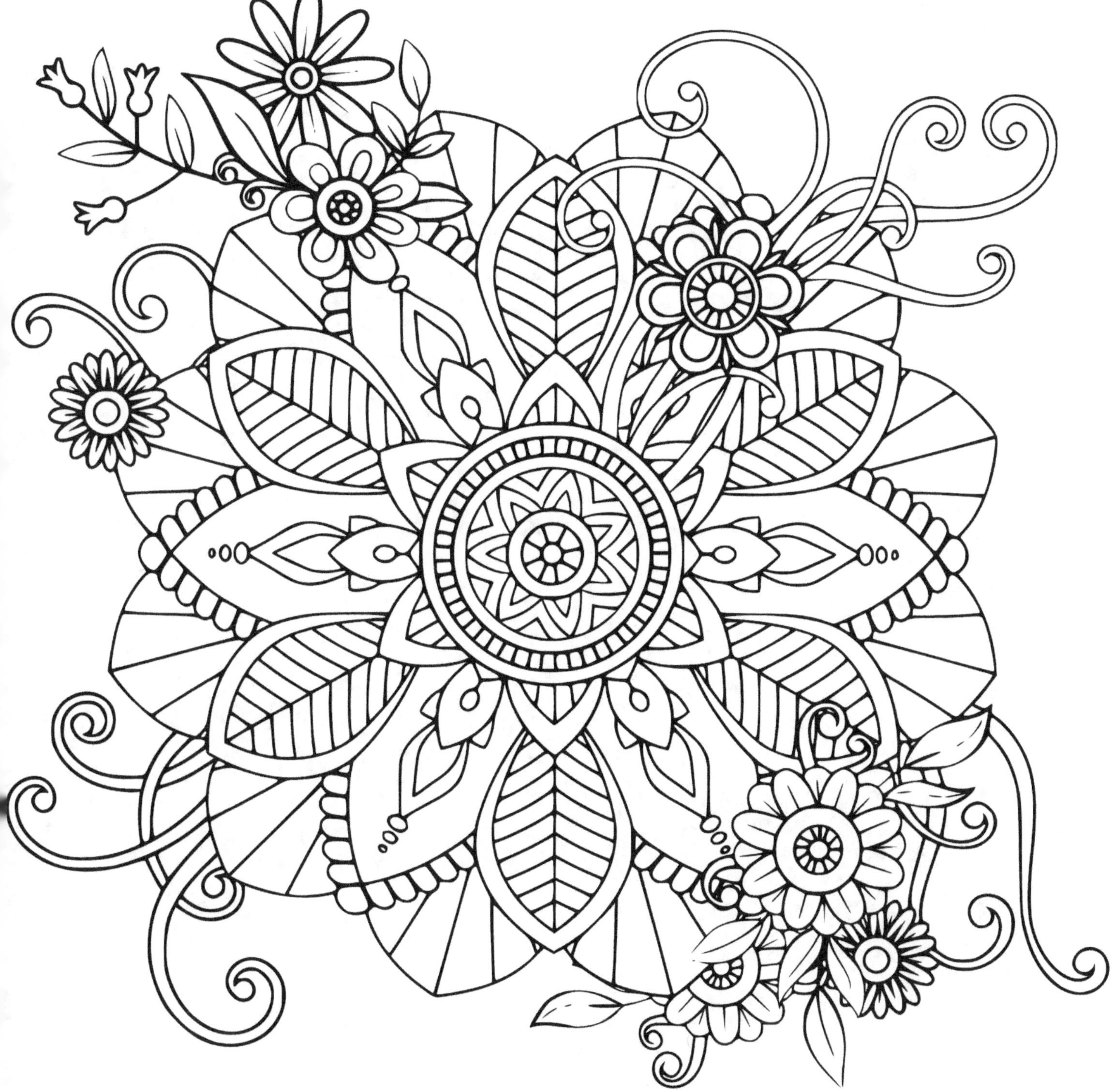

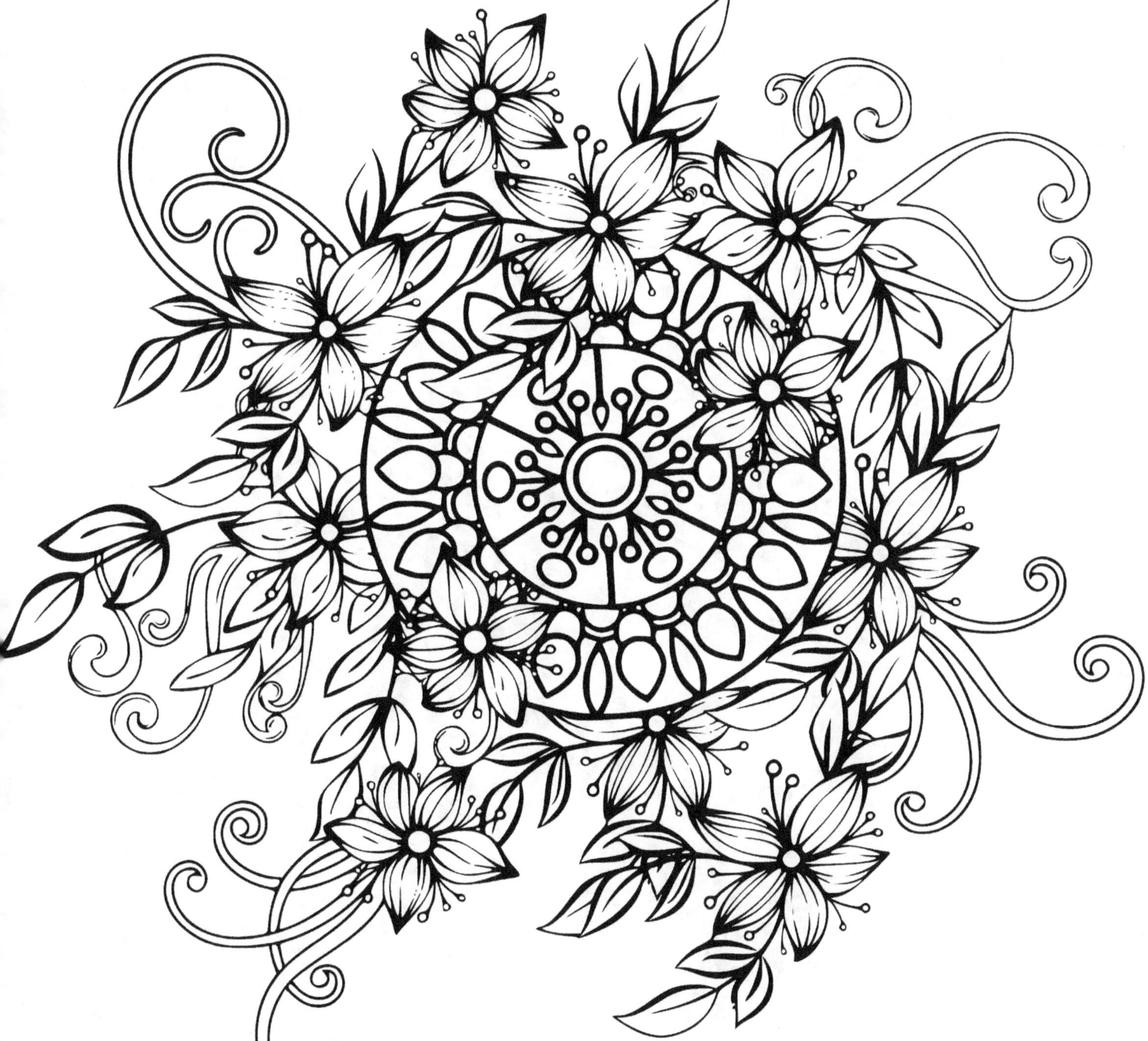

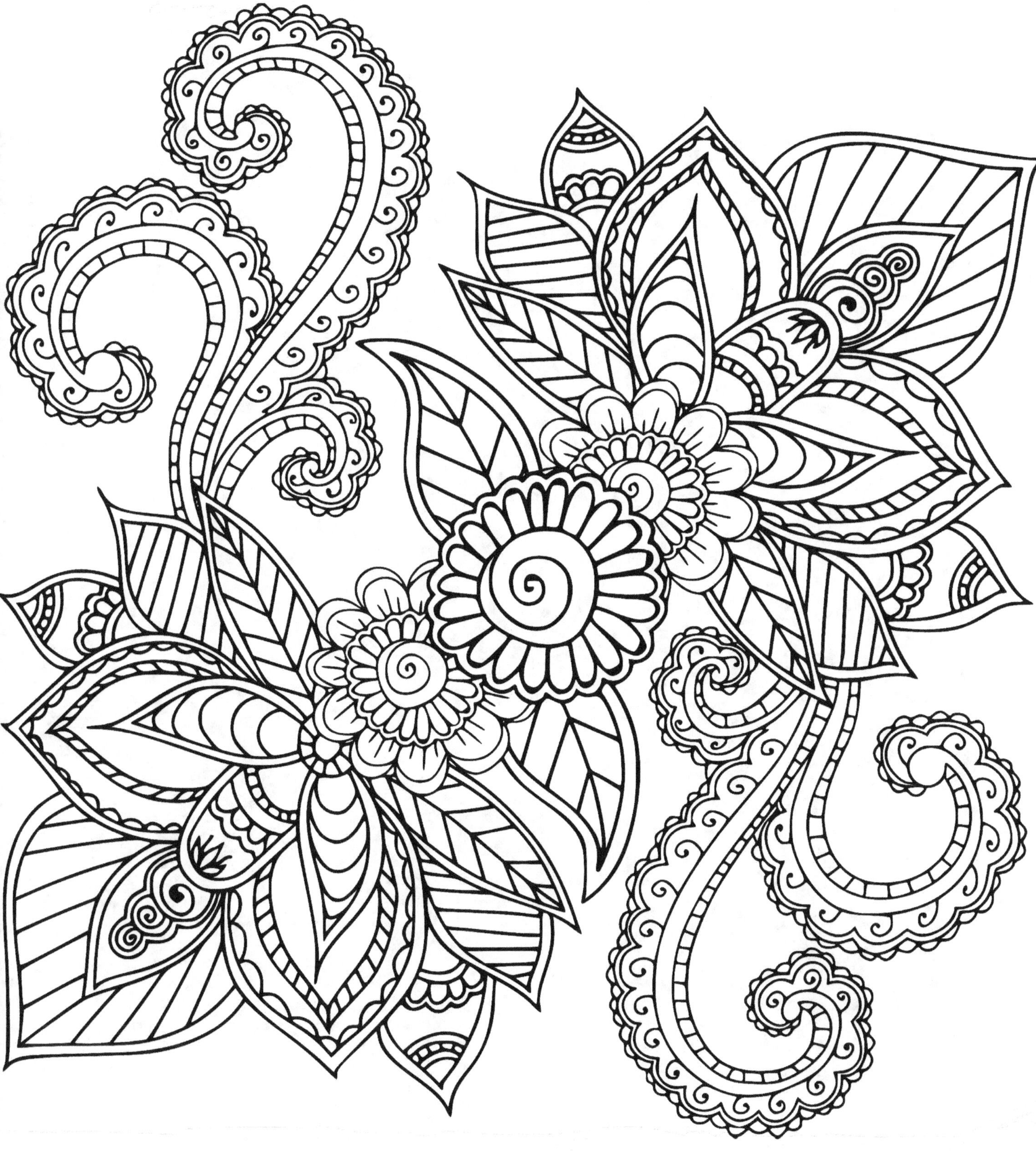

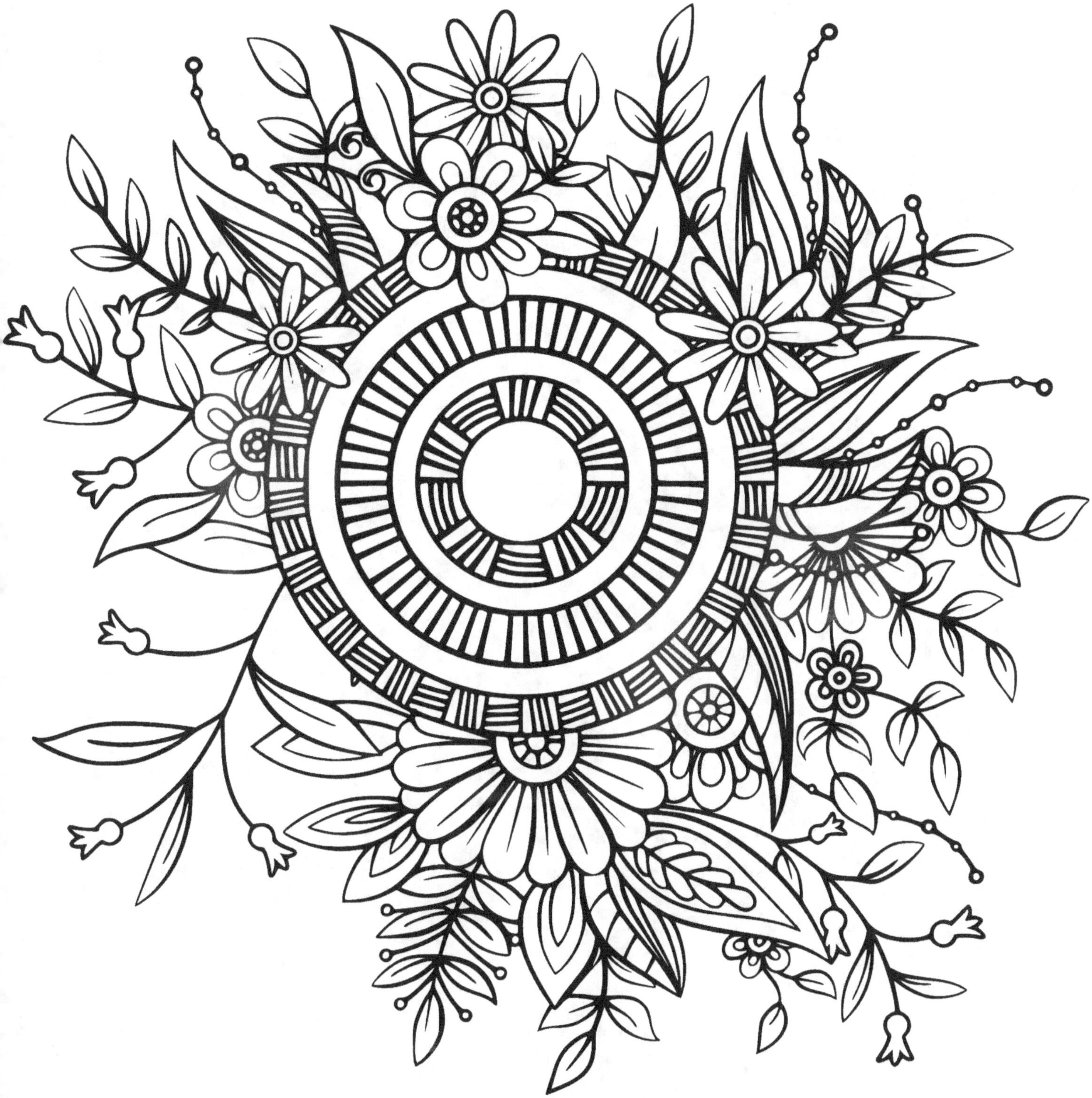

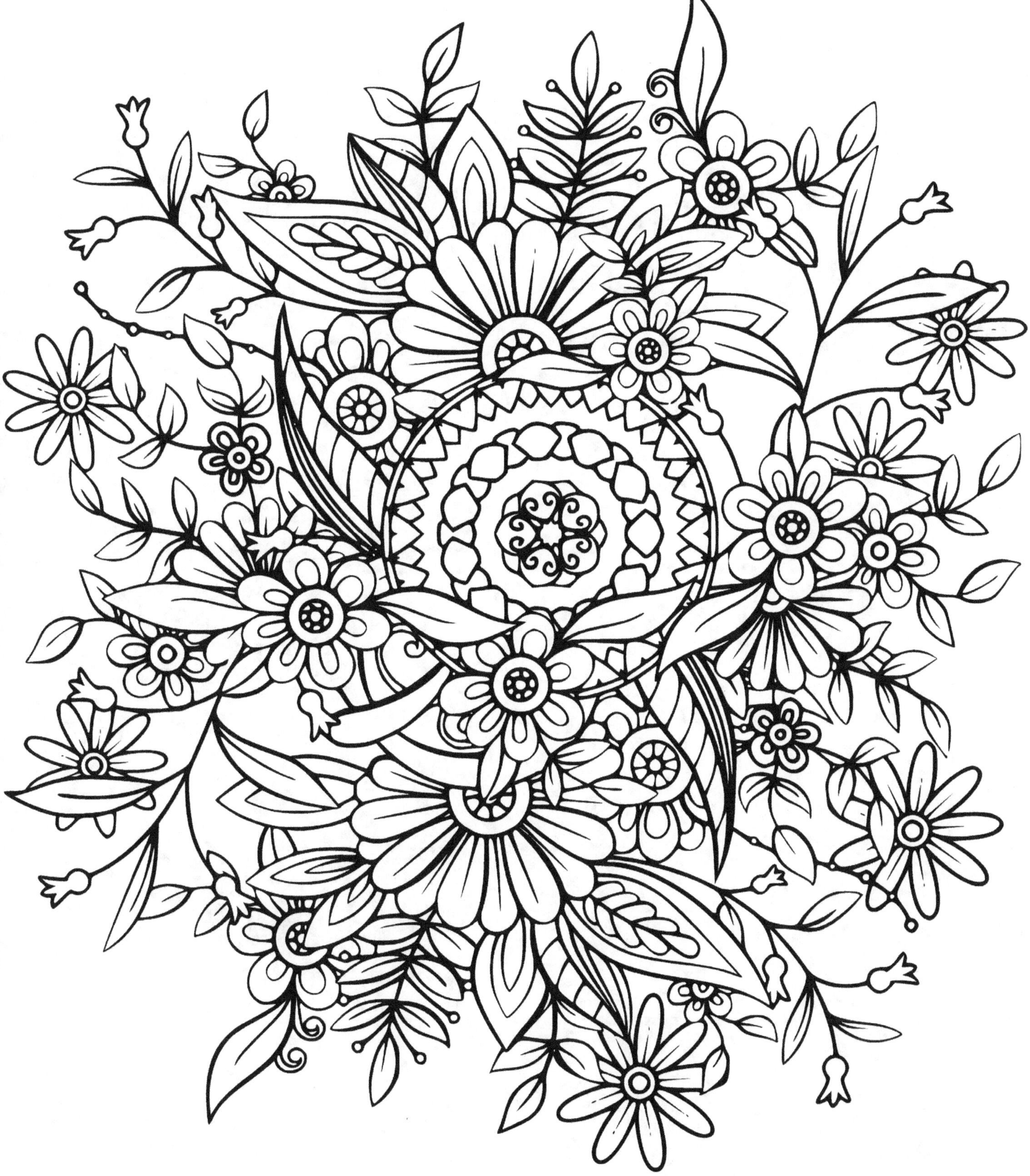

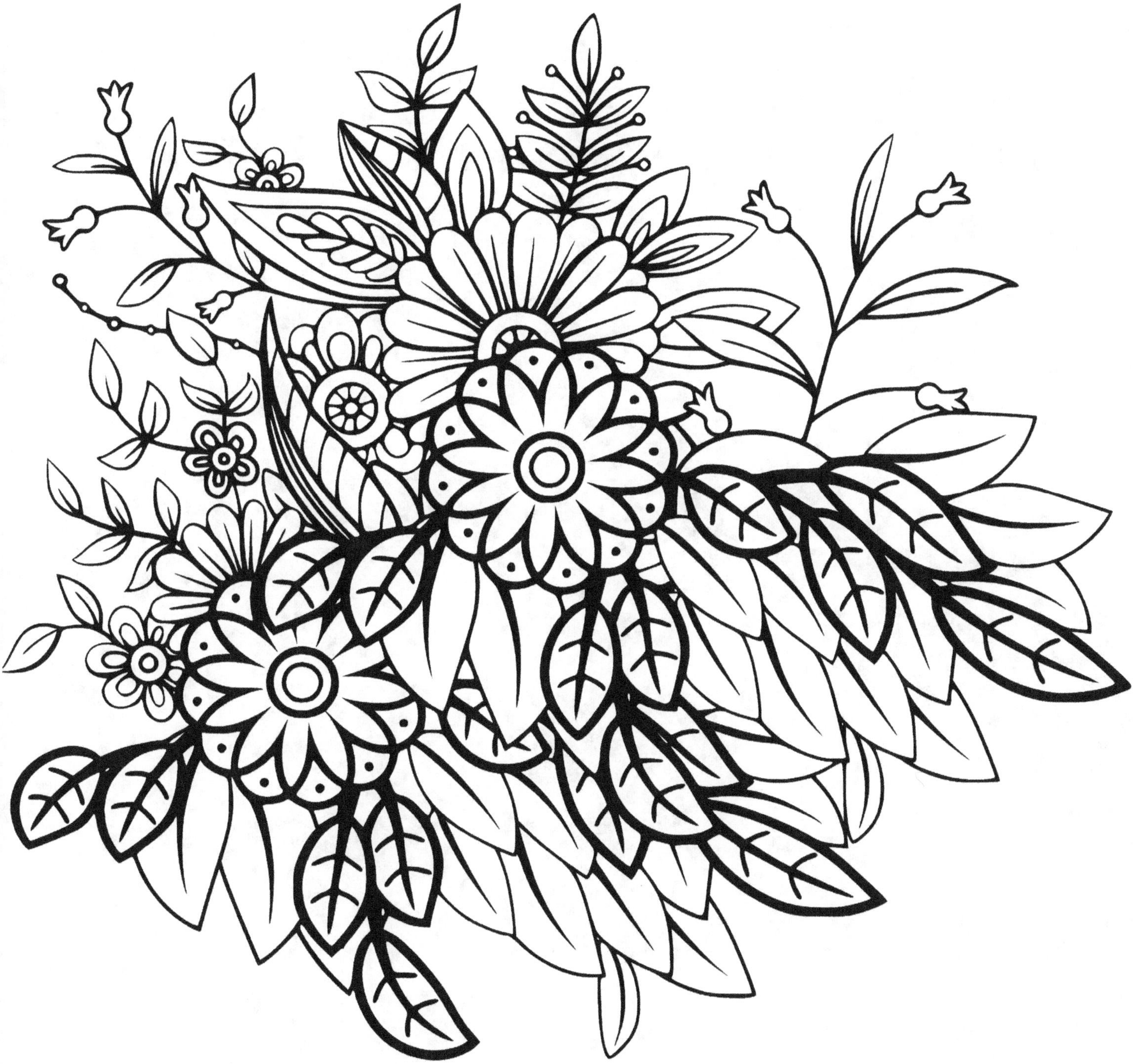

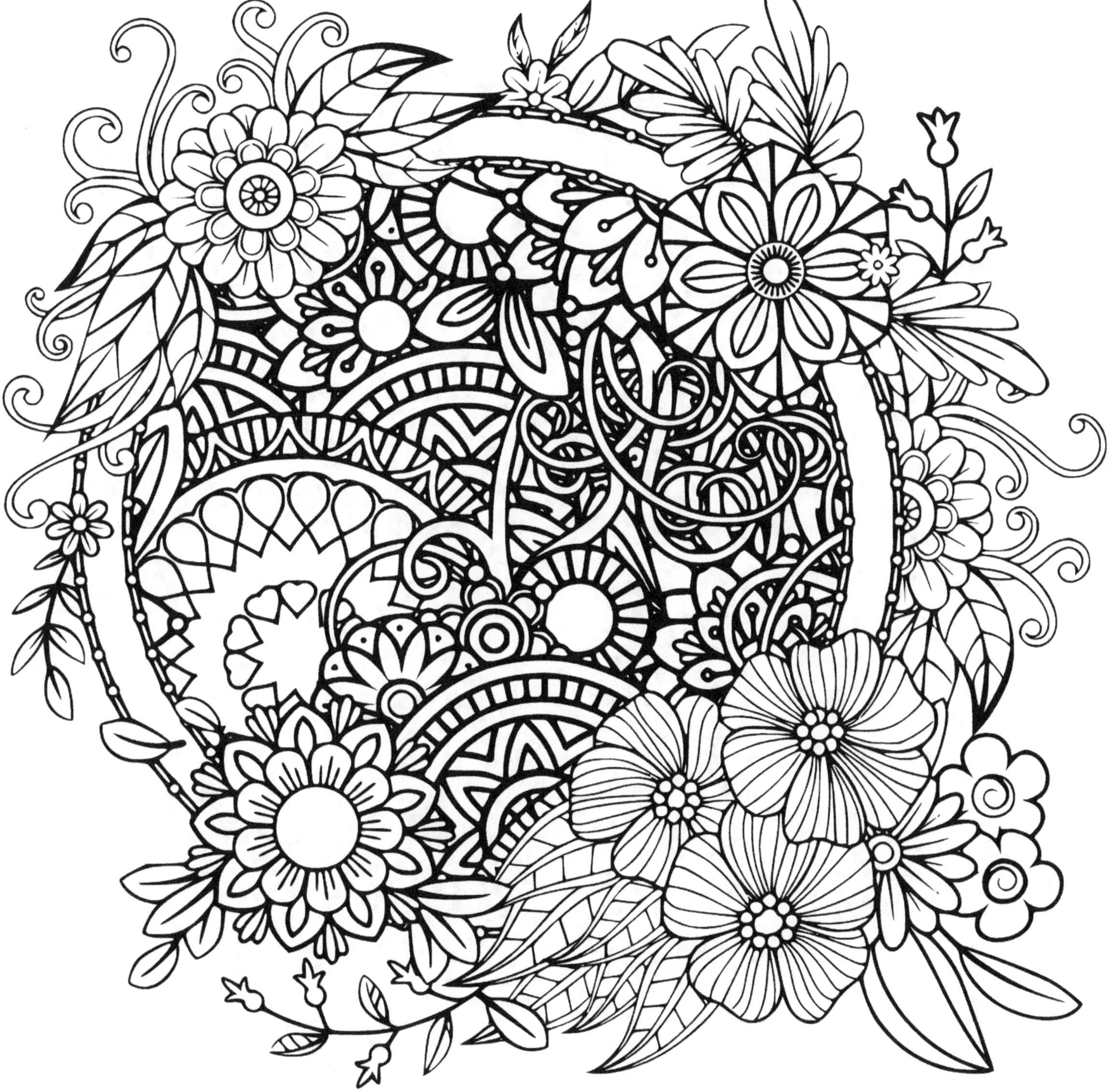

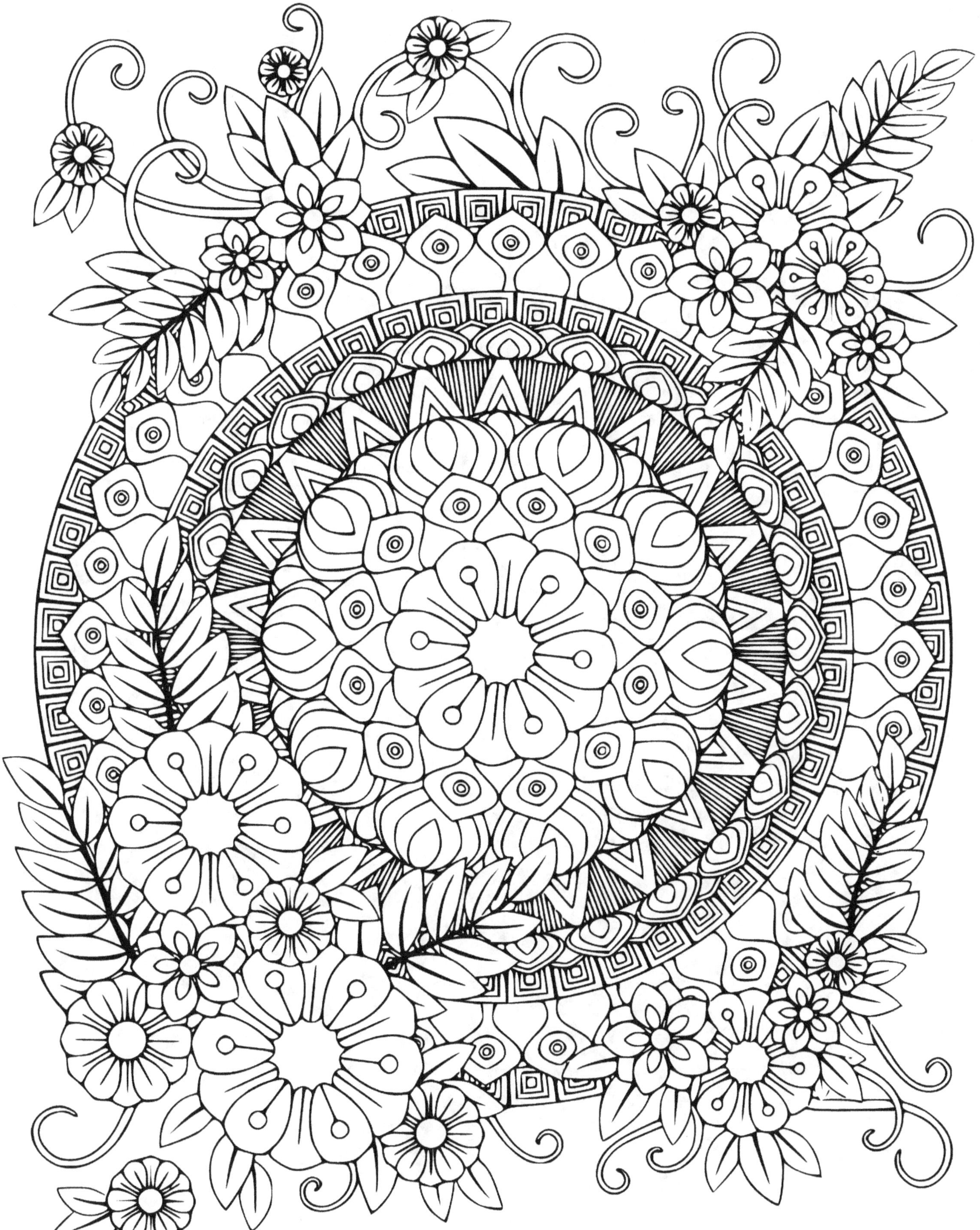

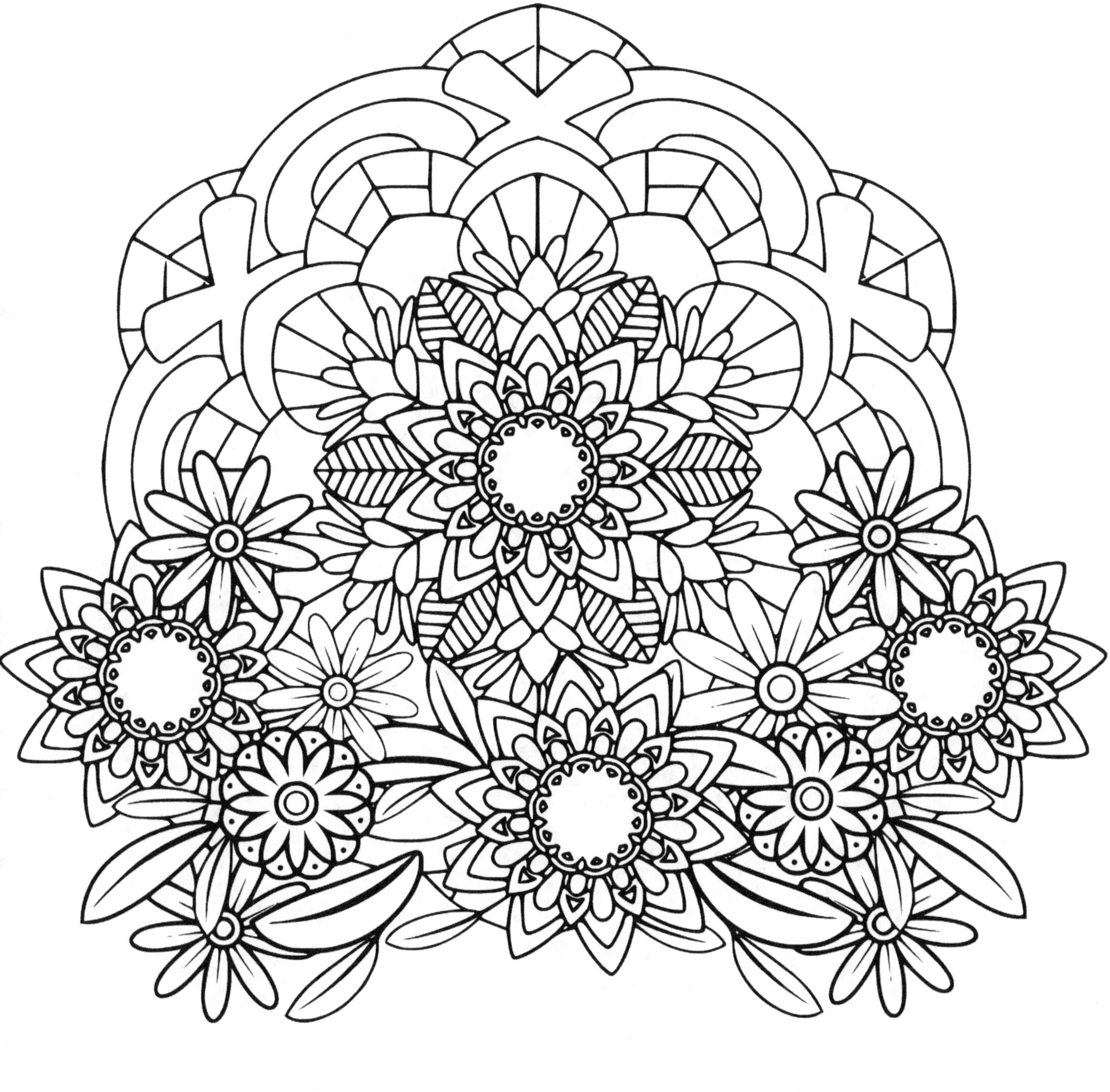

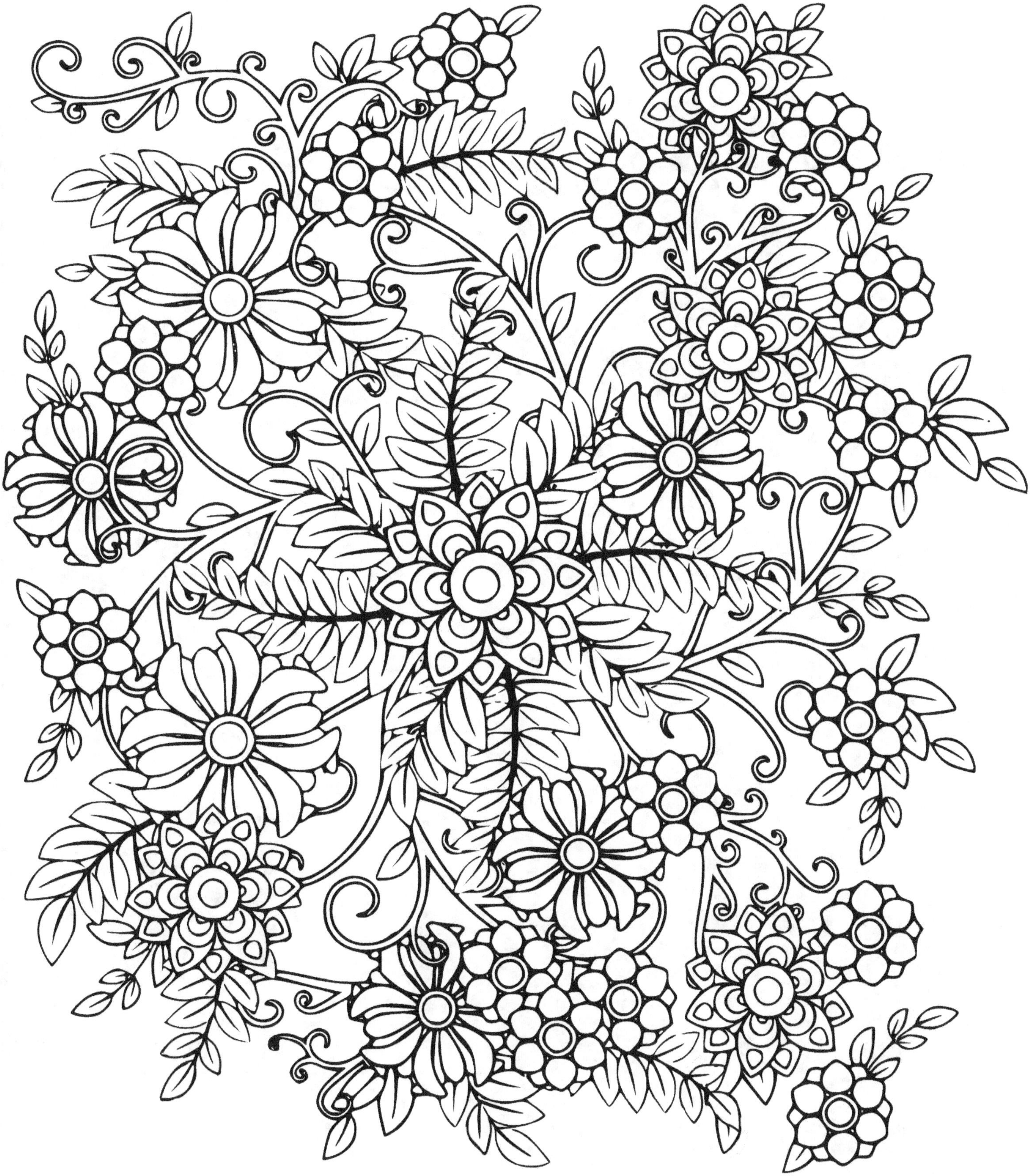

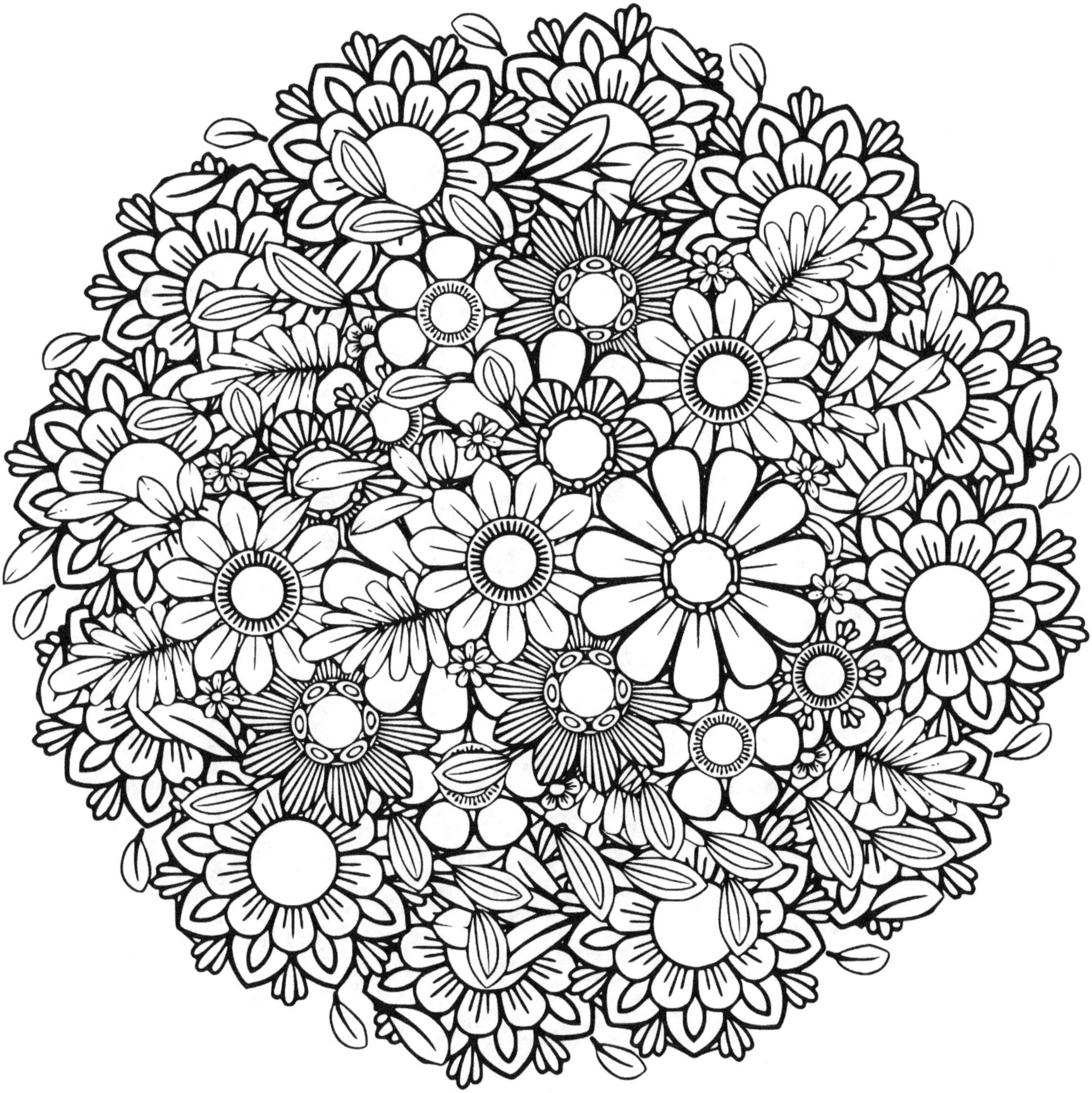

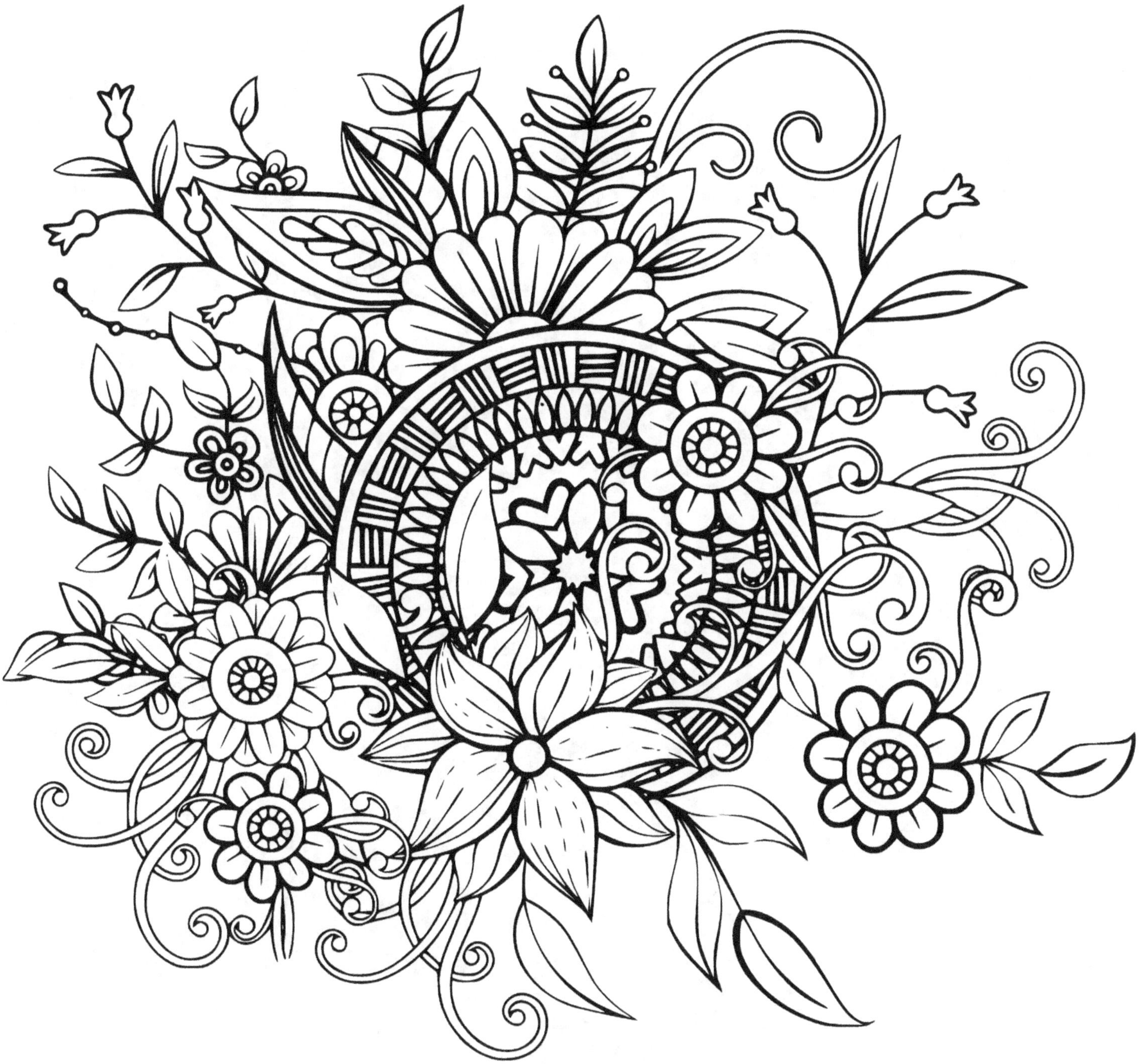

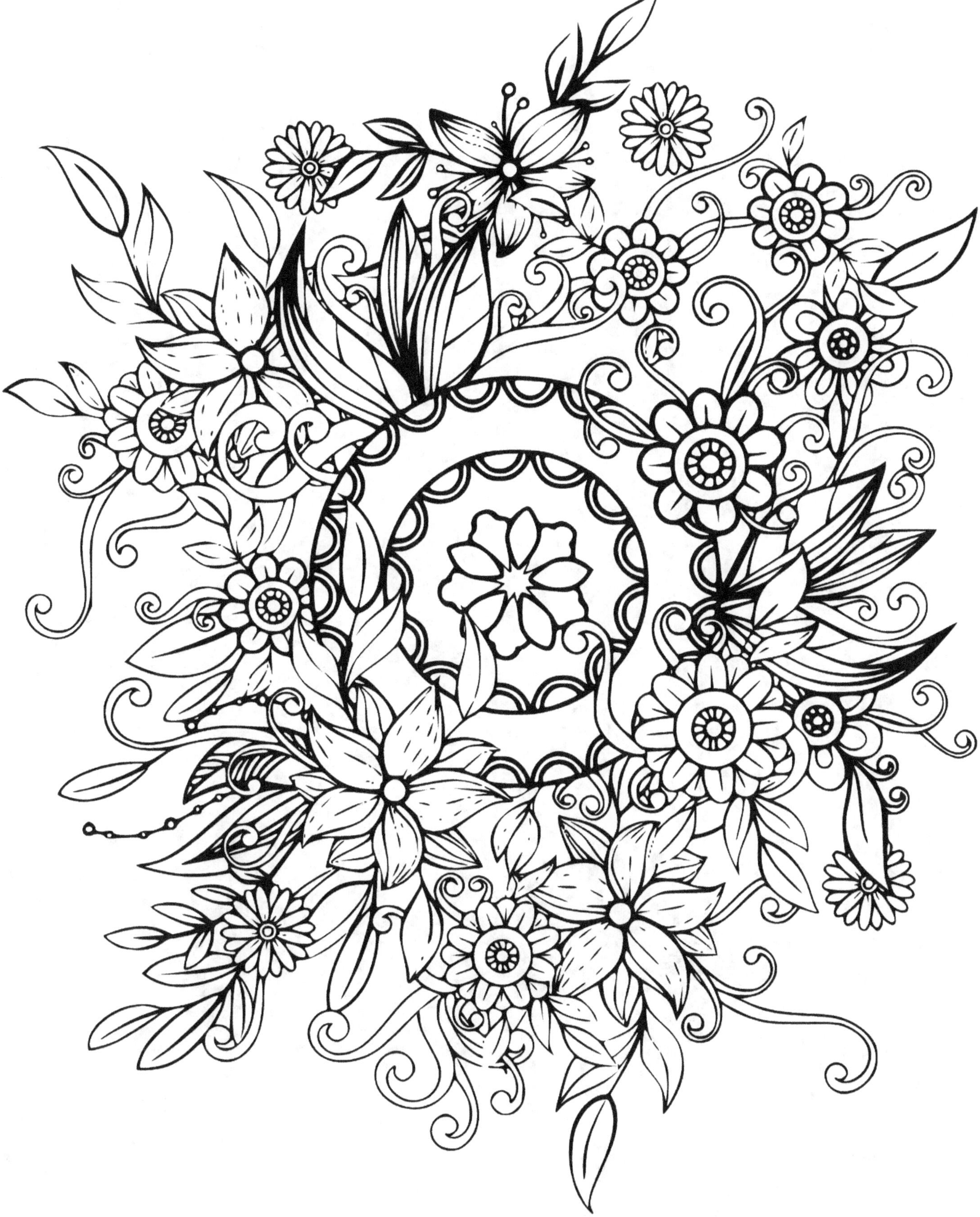

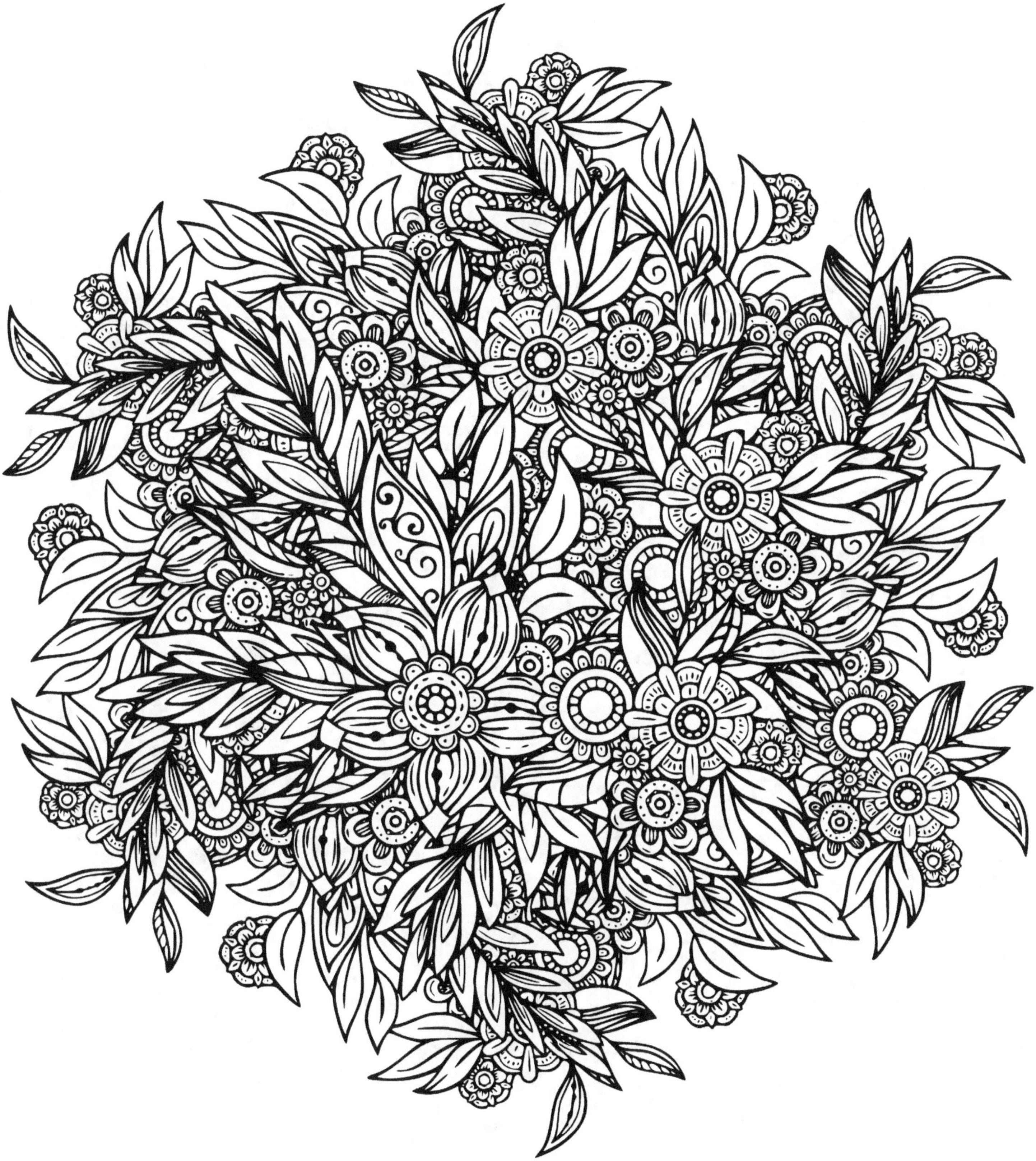

www.ingramcontent.com/pod-product-compliance
Lightning Source LLC
Chambersburg PA
CBHW081655220526
45466CB00009B/2767
* 9 7 8 1 6 5 5 2 0 4 0 7 4 *